This Book
Belongs To

Scan This

Copyright © Pixelart studio

COLOR TEST

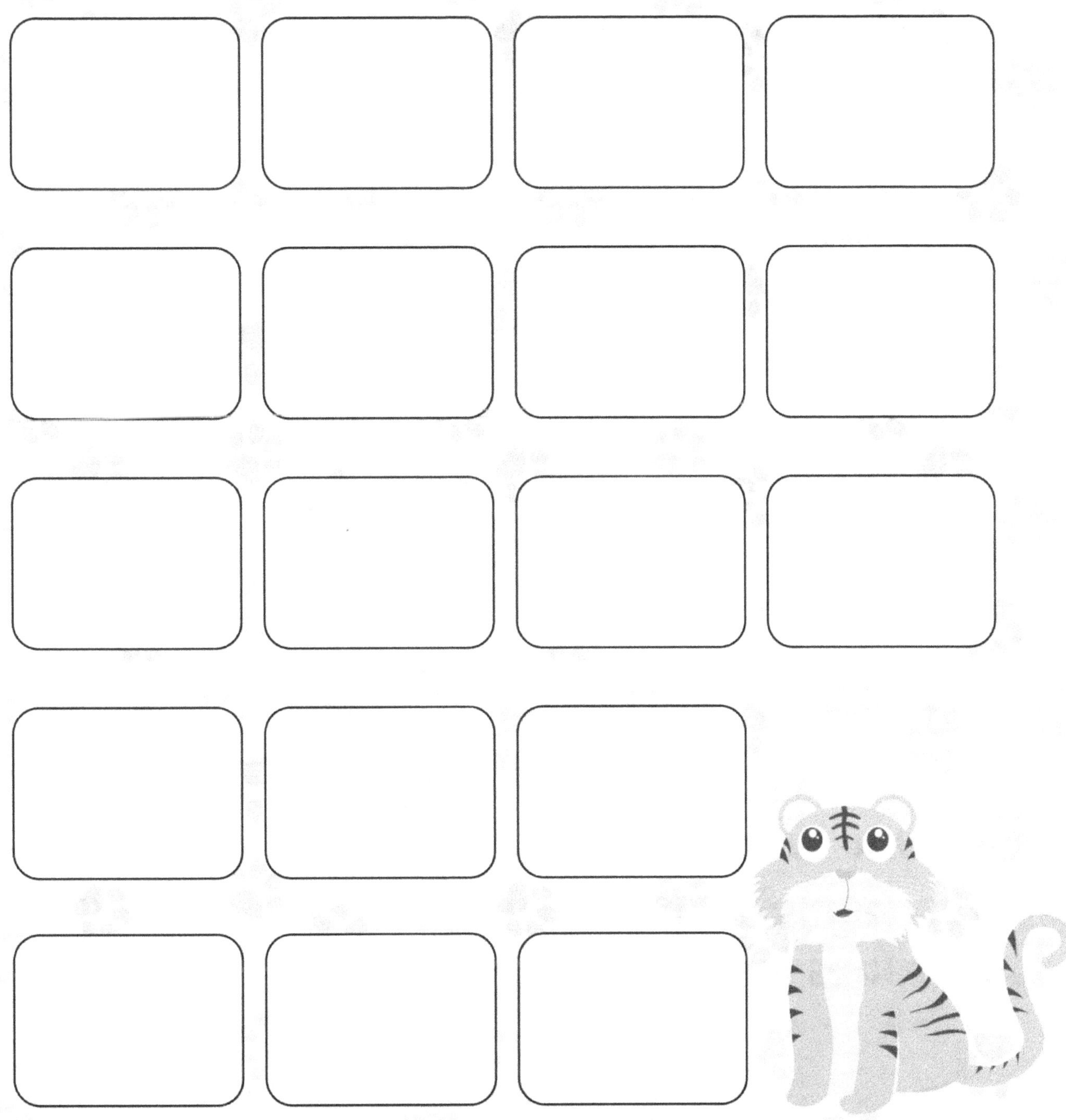

NOTICE!

★ All you need is a pencil, eraser and color.

★ It's not necessary to pick real life color, pick whatever color you like most. You can even mix colors!

★ Draw lightly at first. Add details according to the diagrams, but don't worry about being perfect!

★ Sometimes colors appear differently than you expect. The color test page is a great way to try out colors and shading beforehand.

★ Start on an image whatever you feel comfortable. There's no wrong place to begin! Don't worry if your drawings don't turn out the way you want to. Just take a break, come to it later. Sometimes drawing the same thing for a few times will help.

NOW LET'S COLOR!

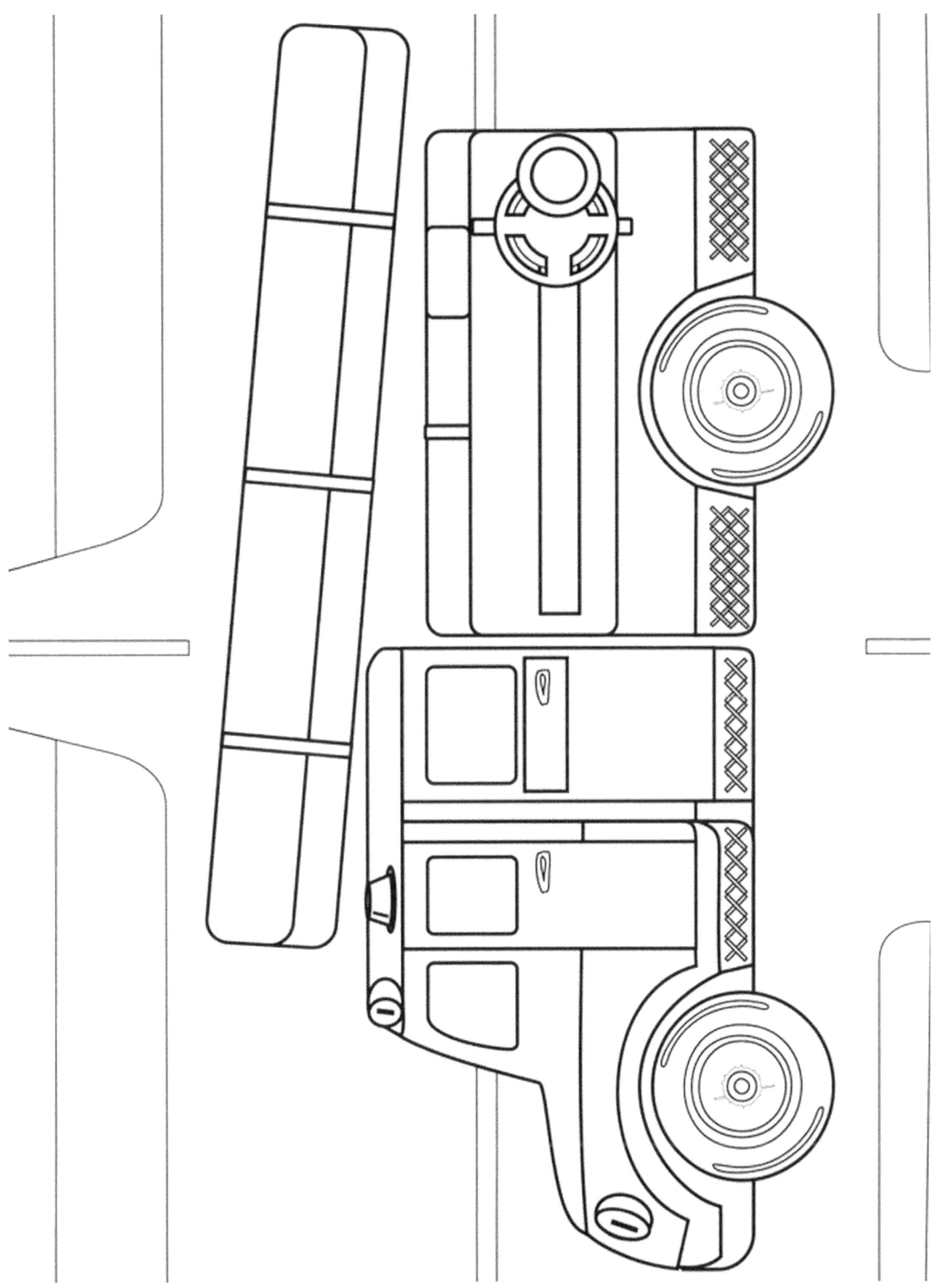

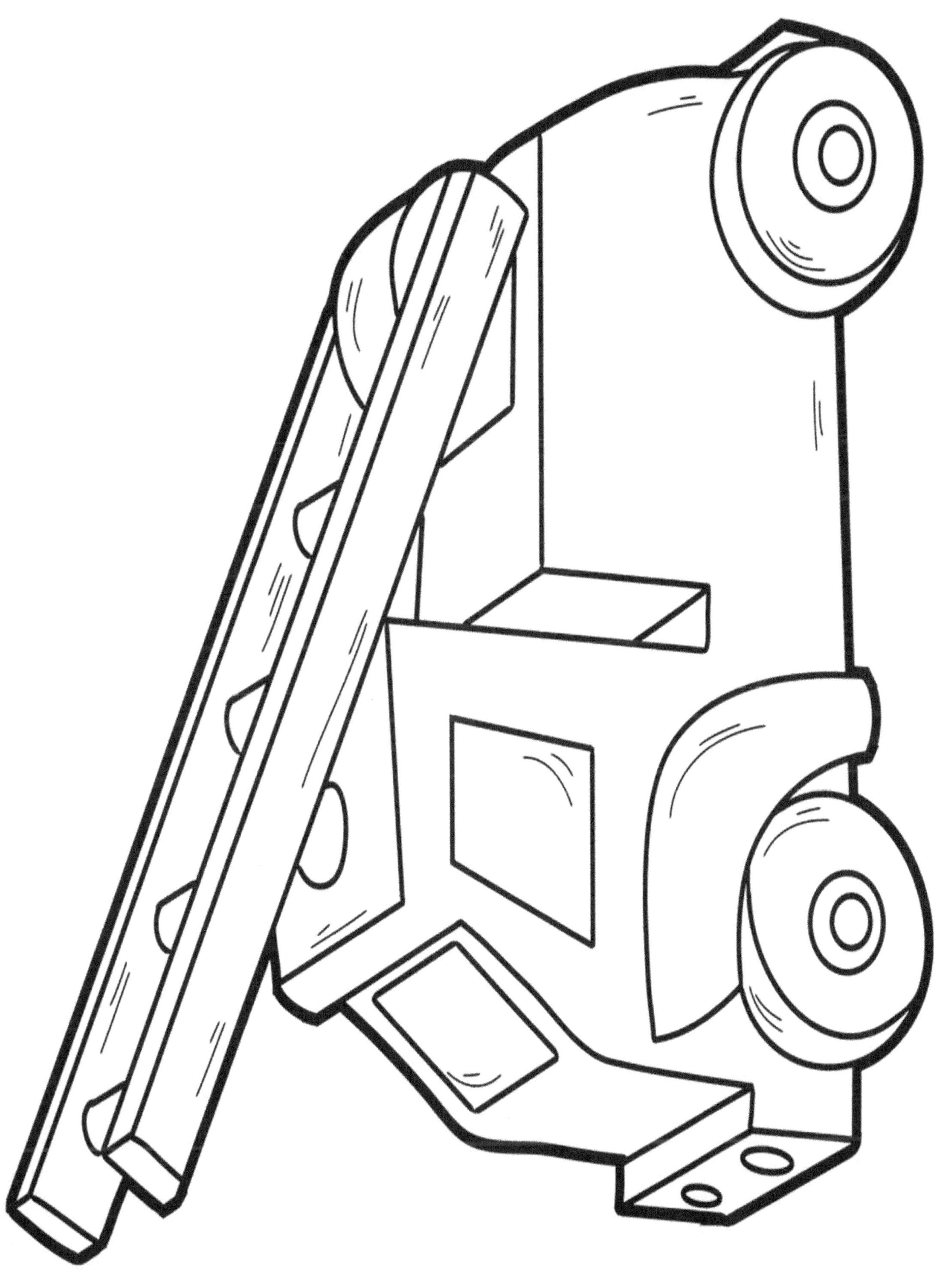

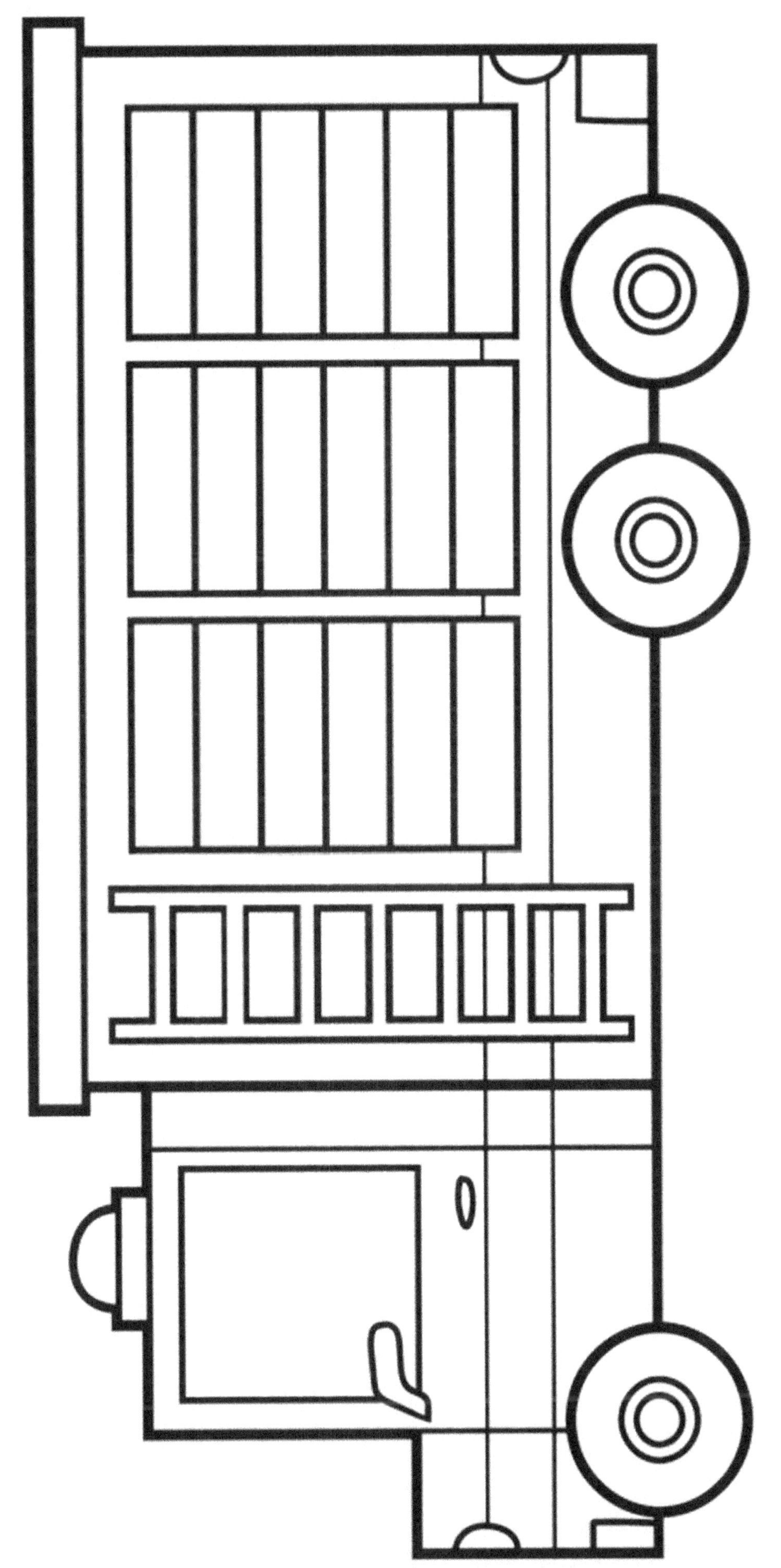

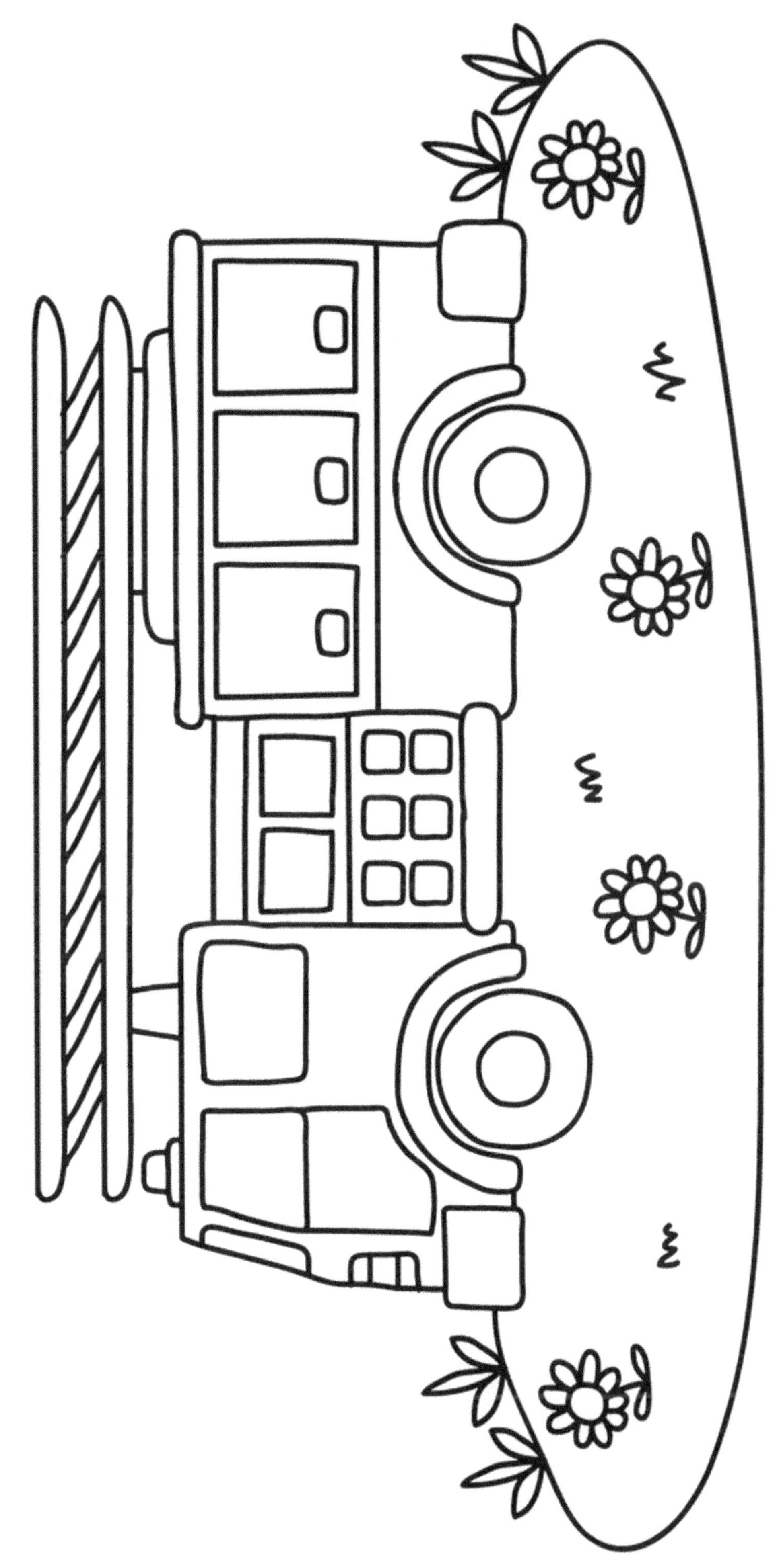

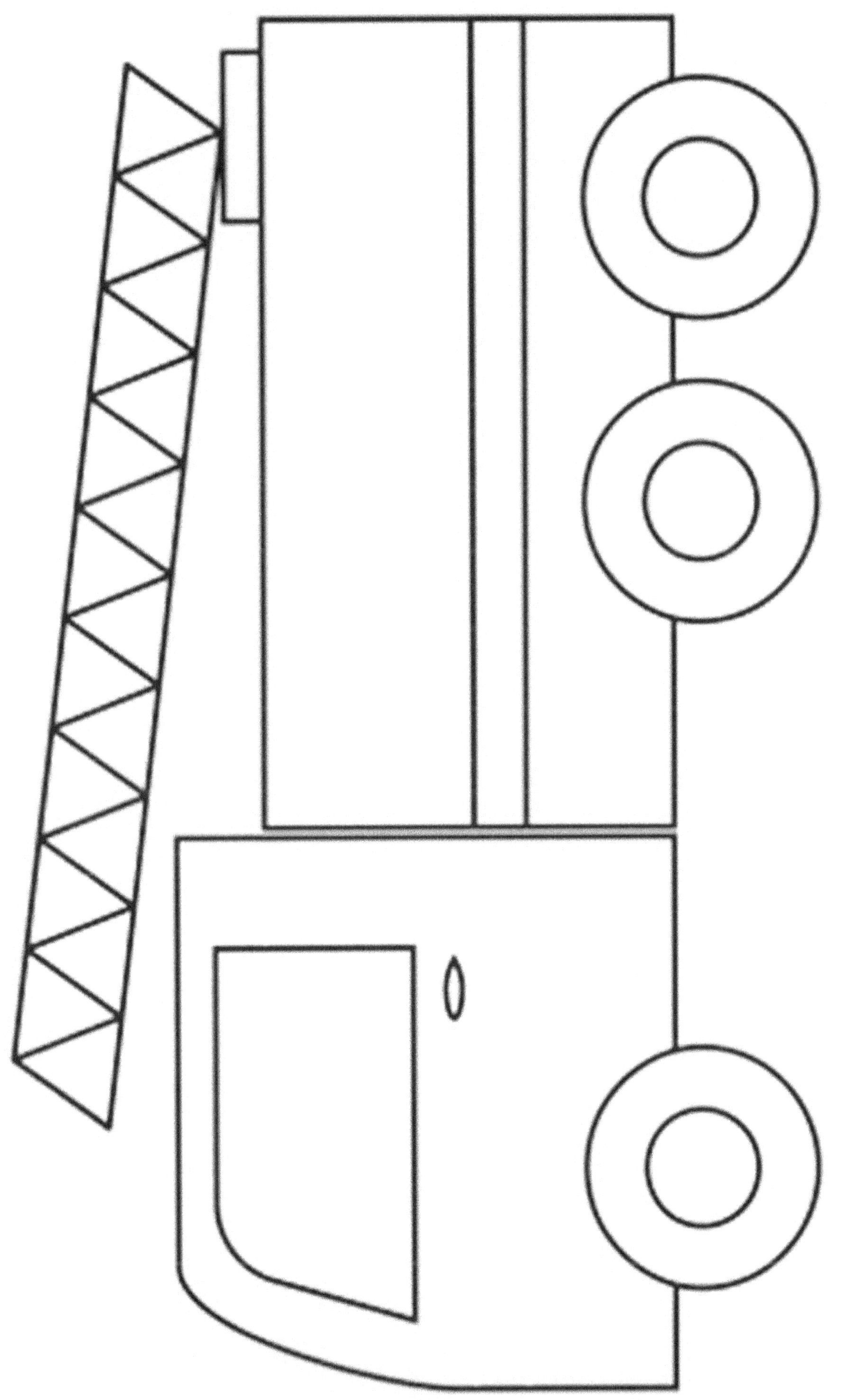

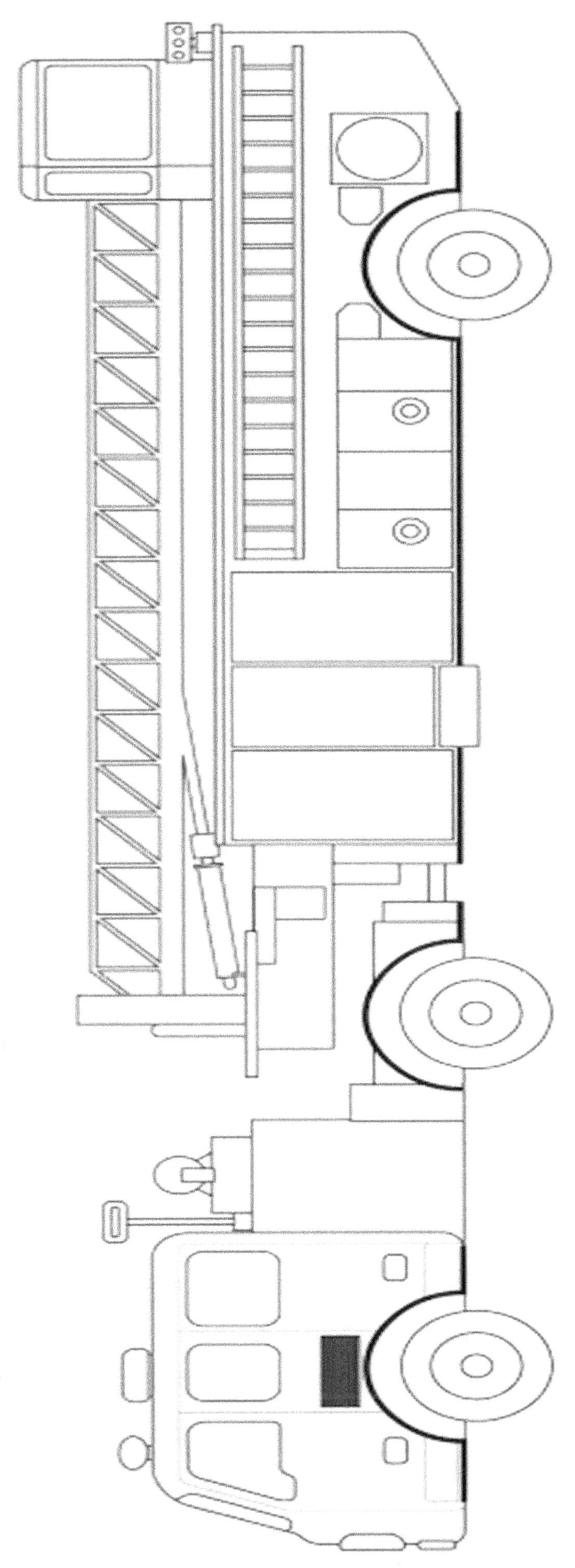

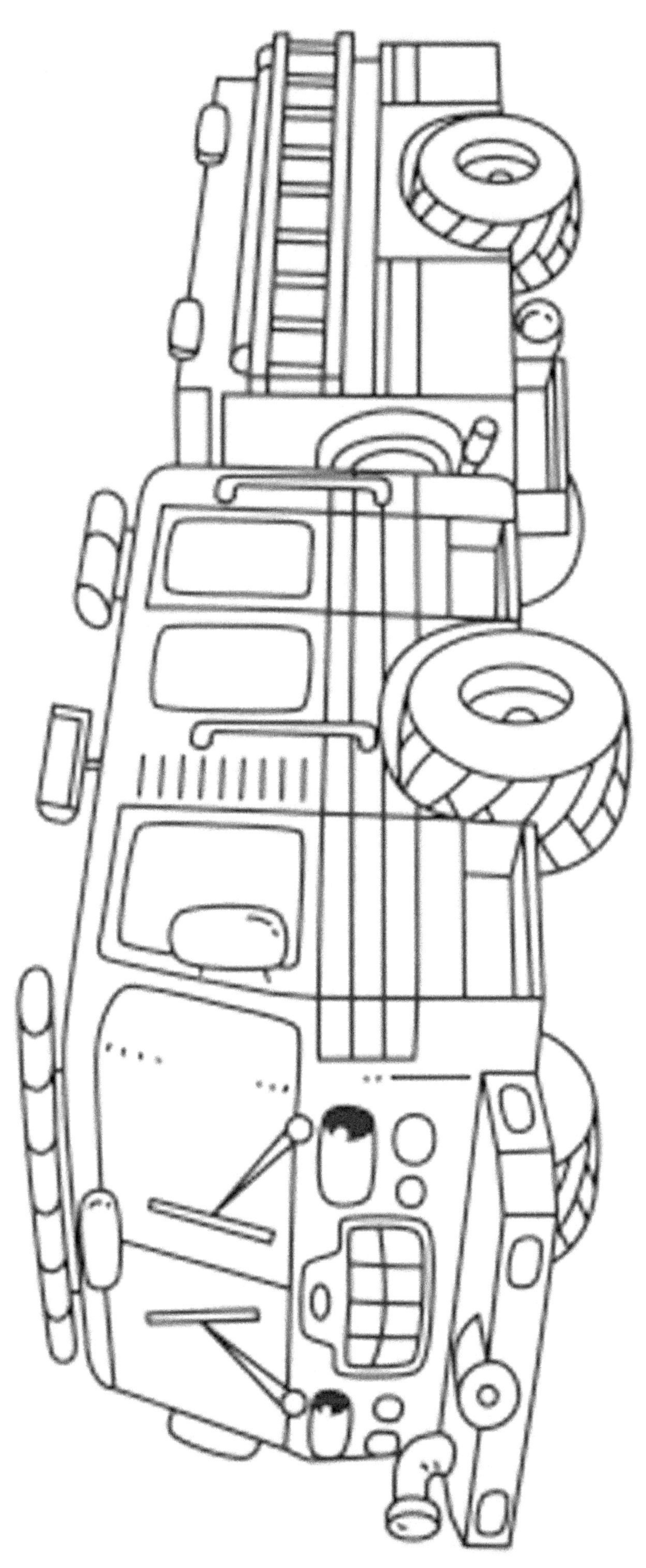

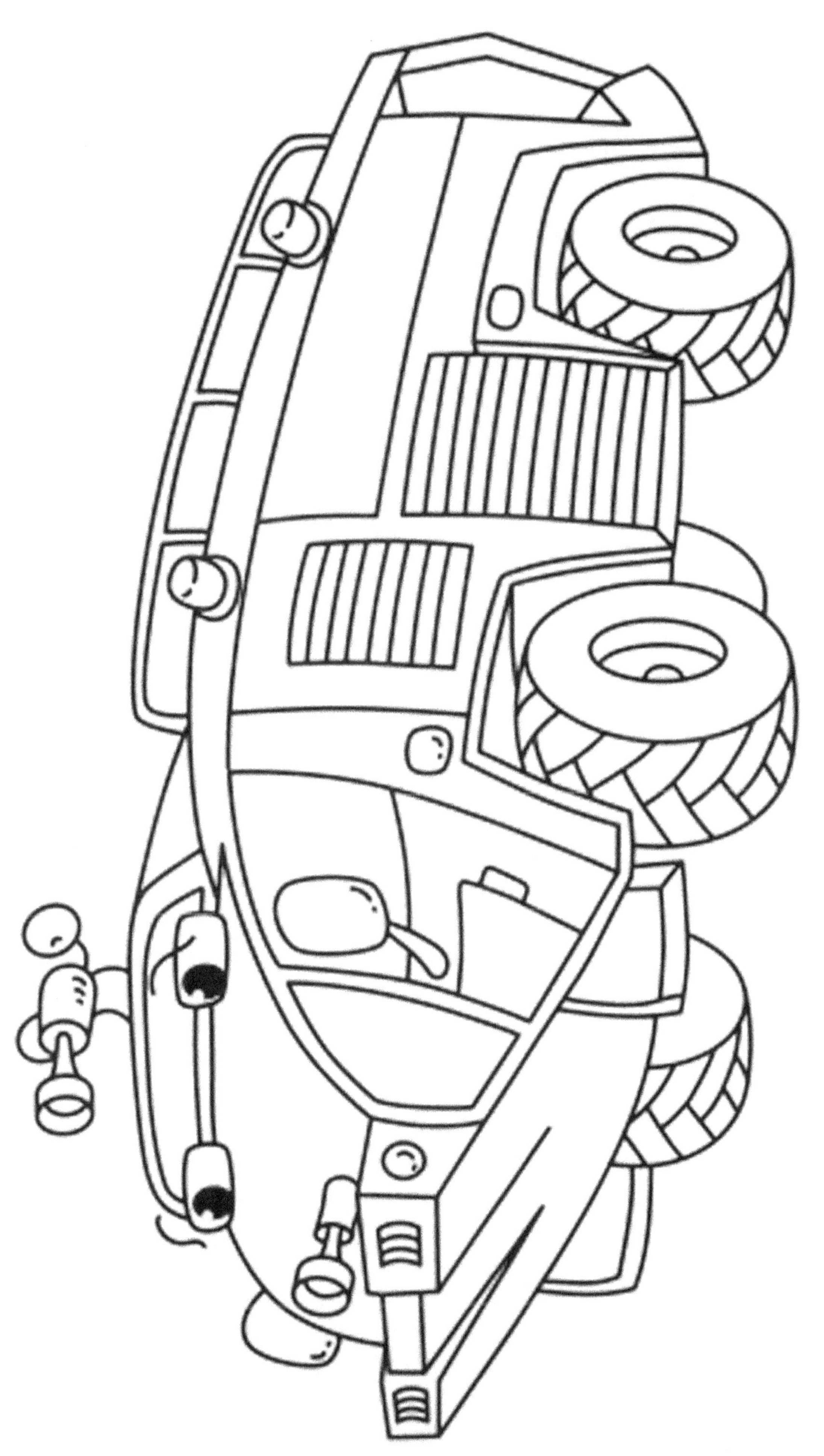

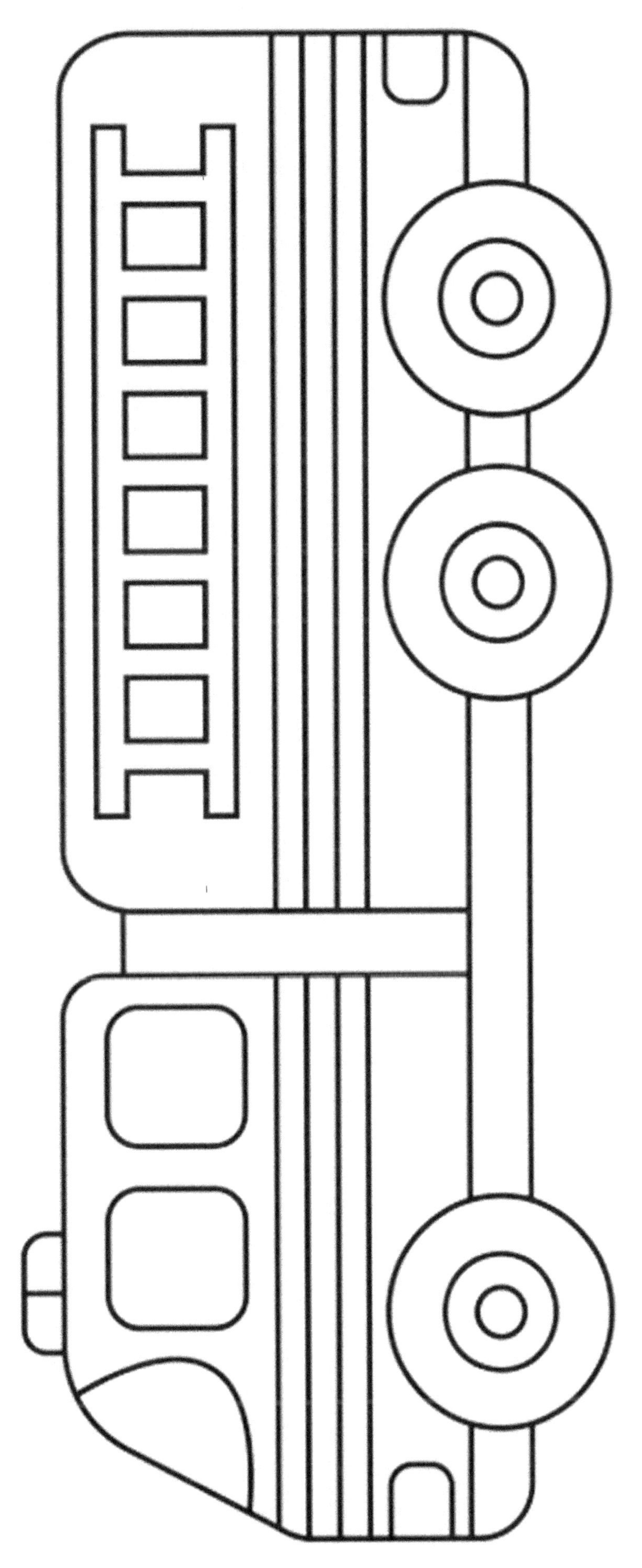

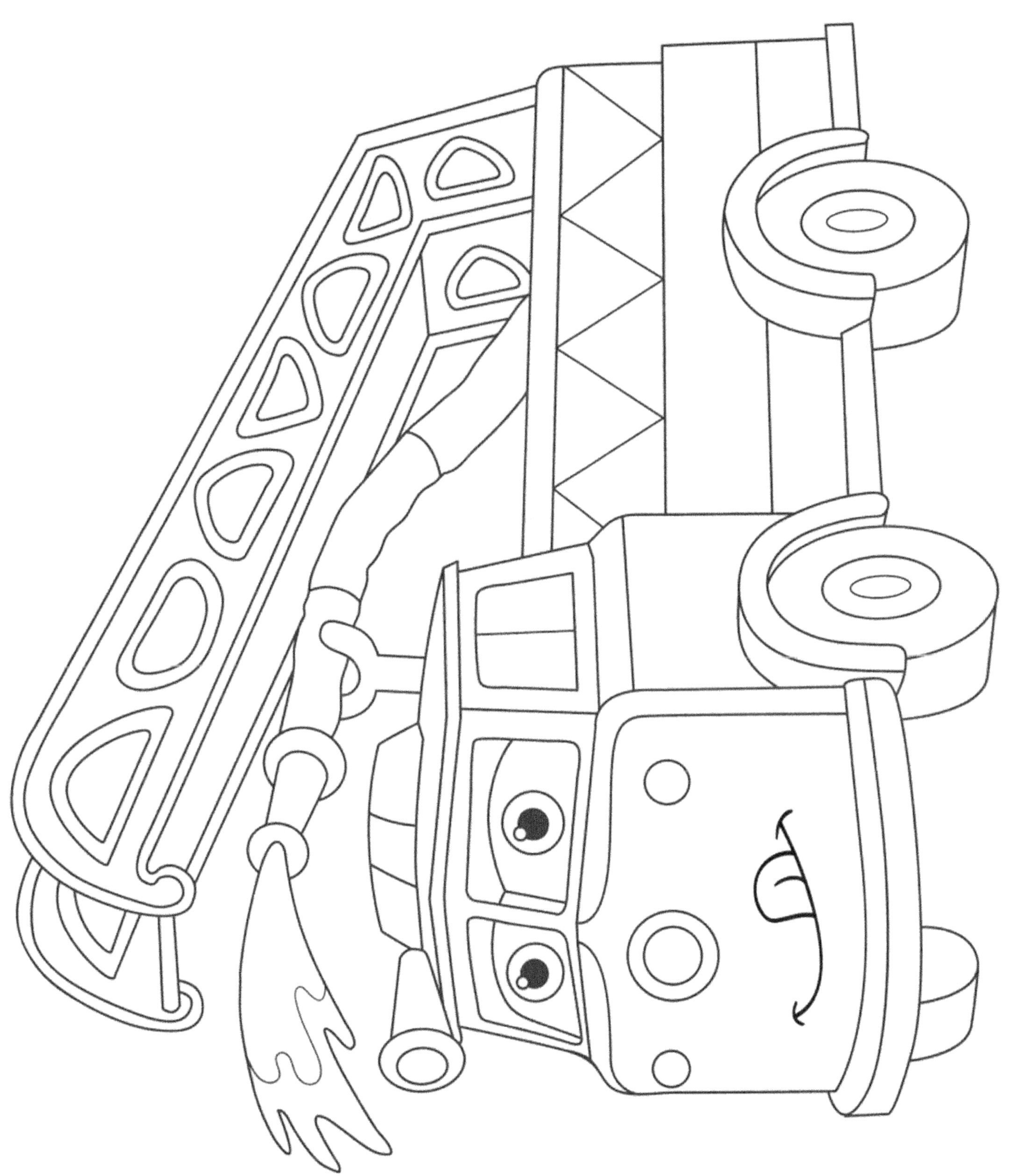

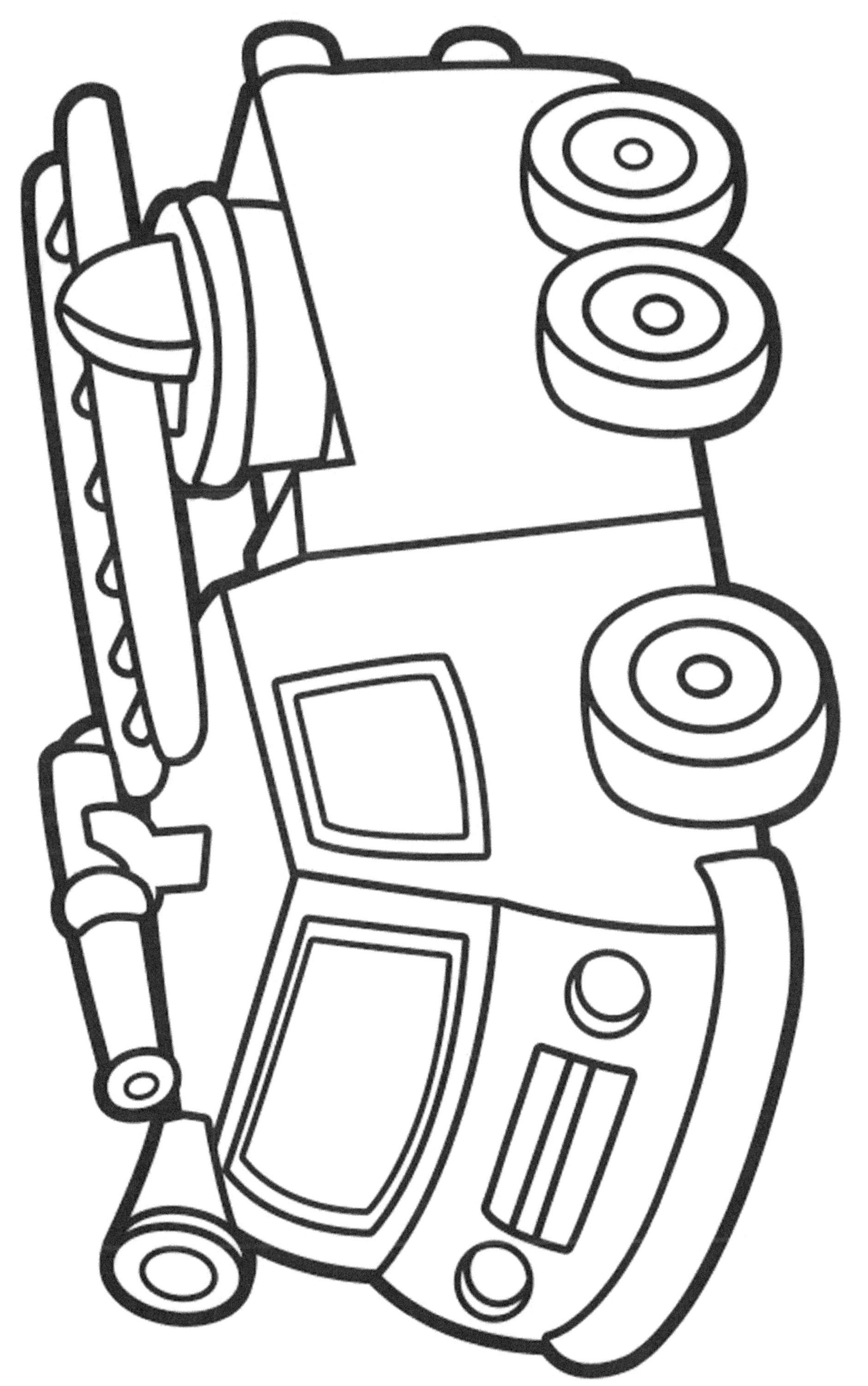

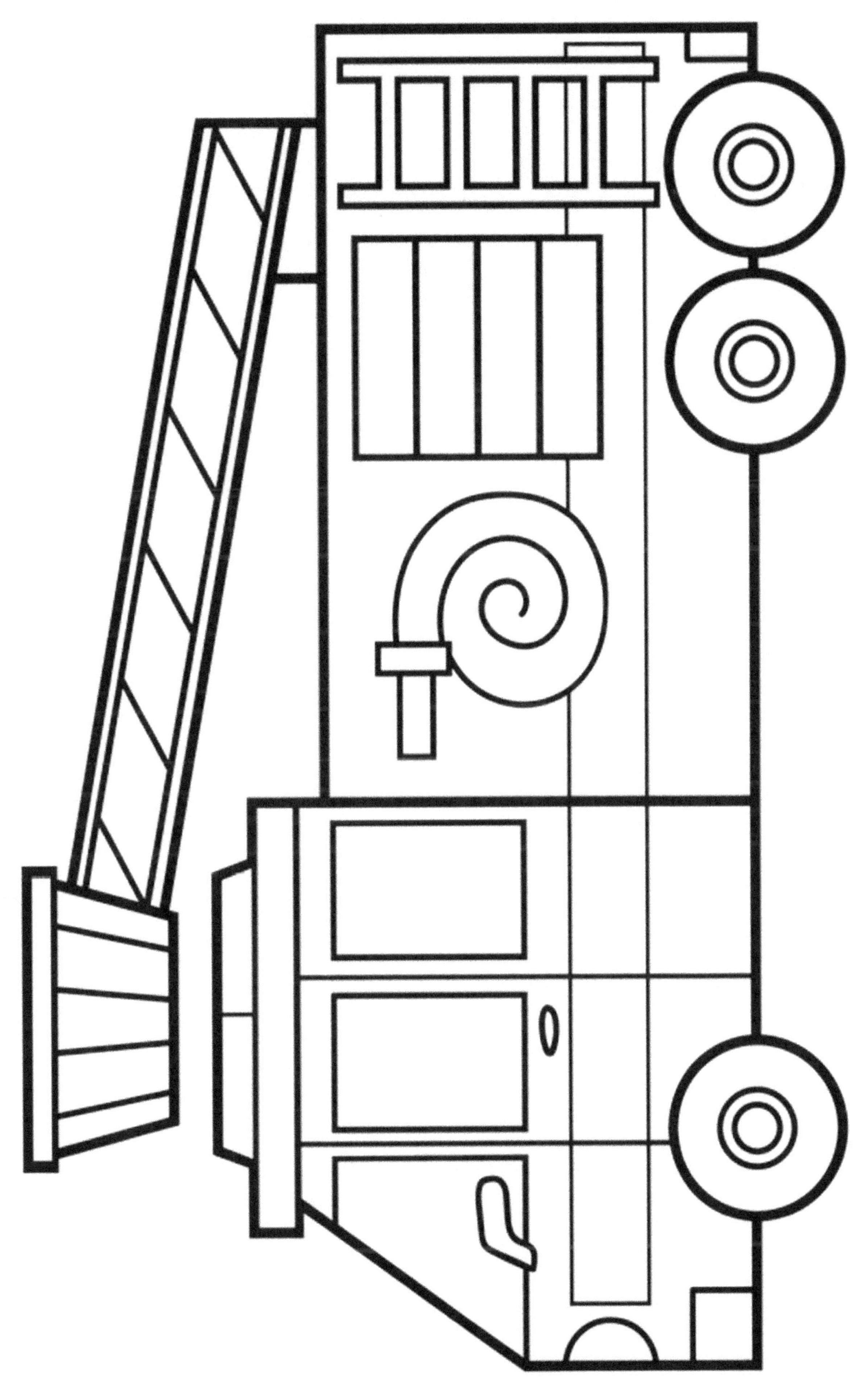

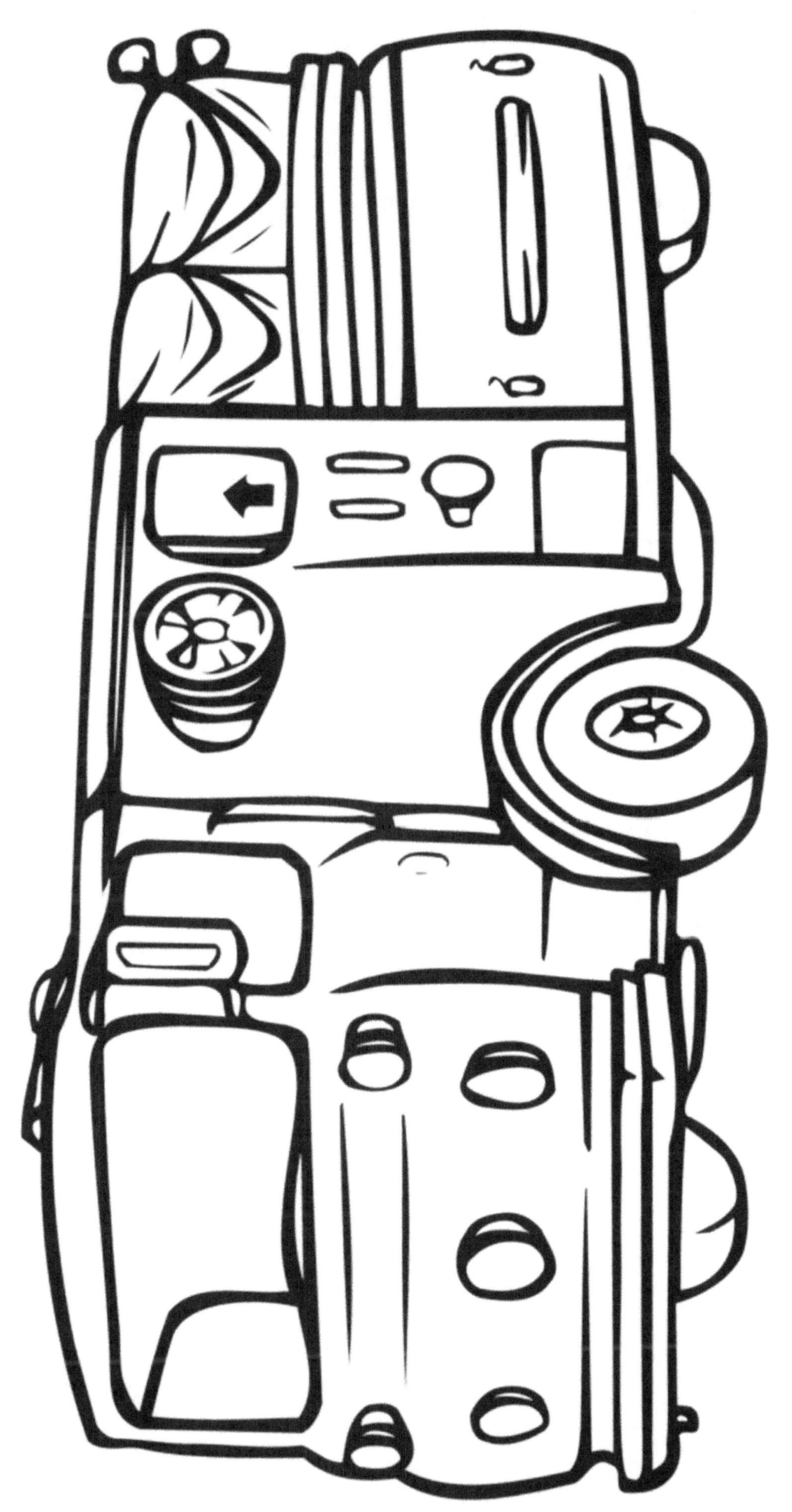

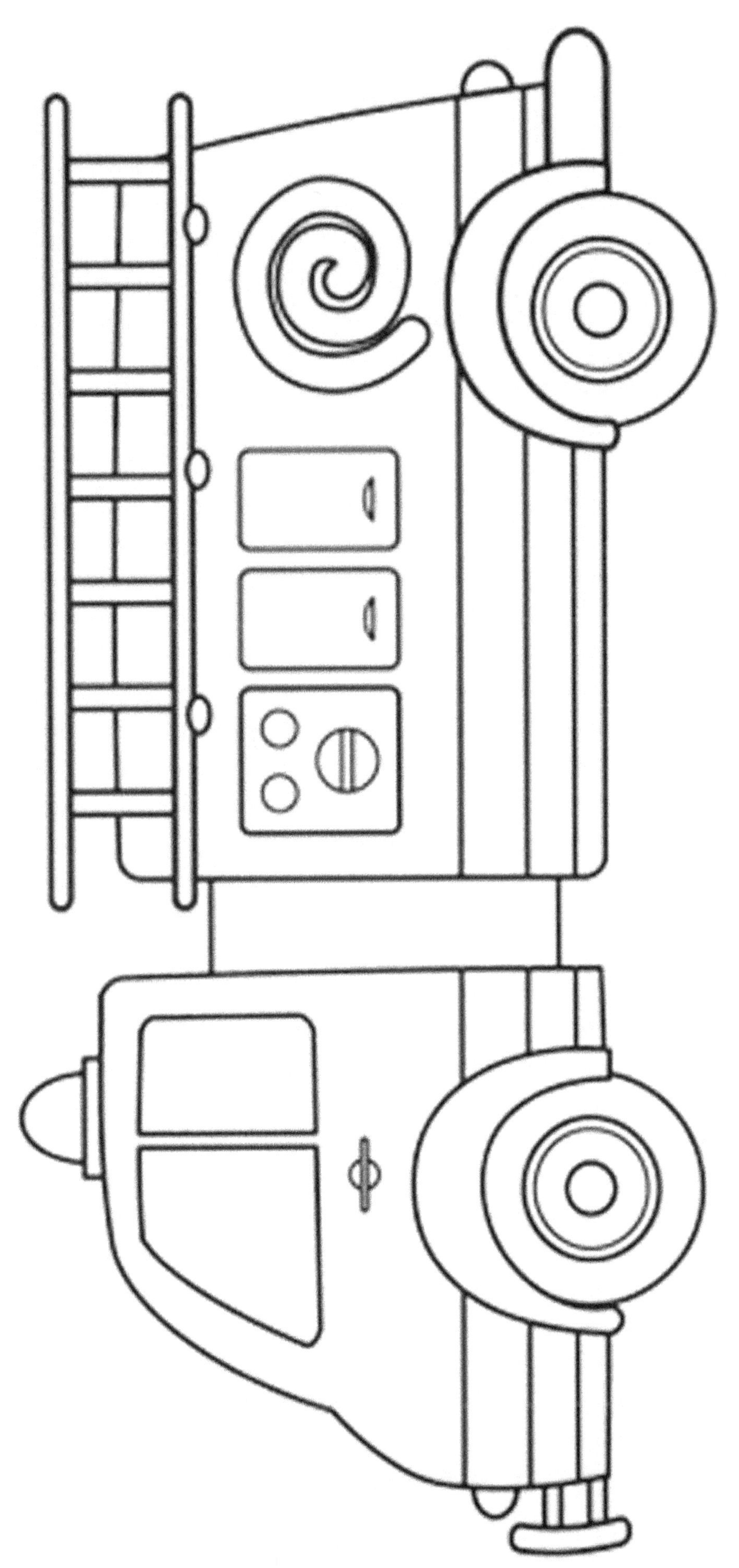

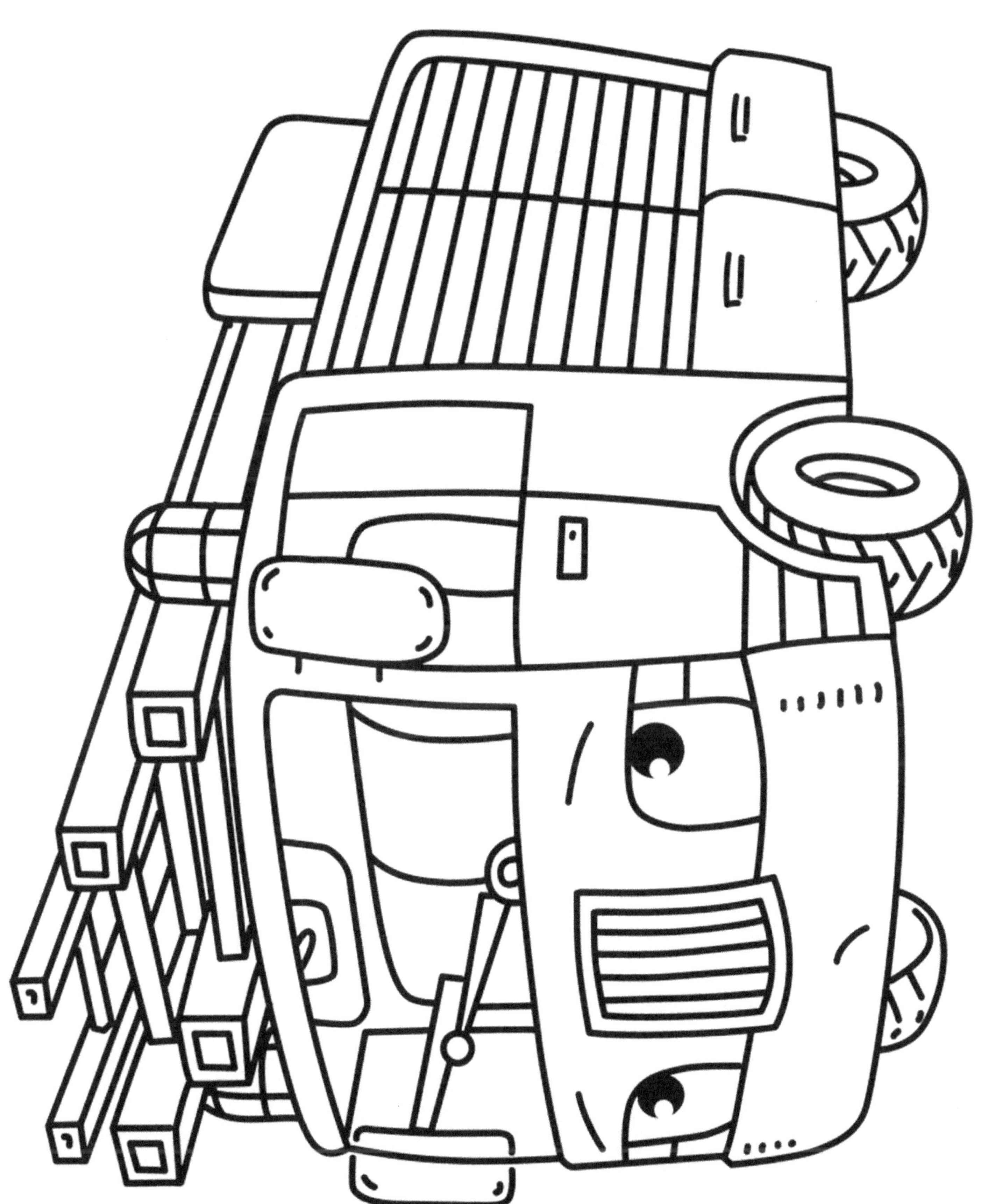

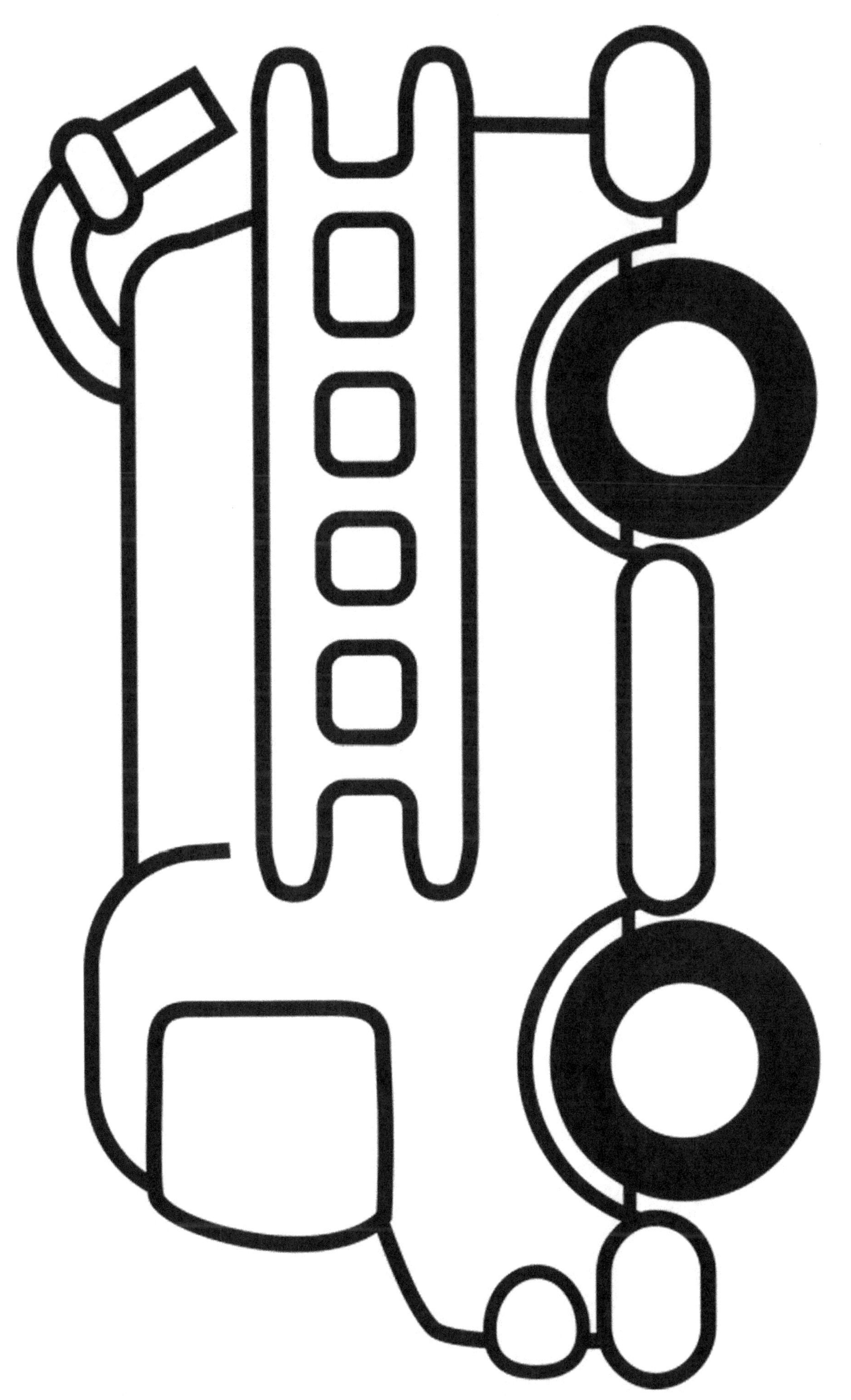

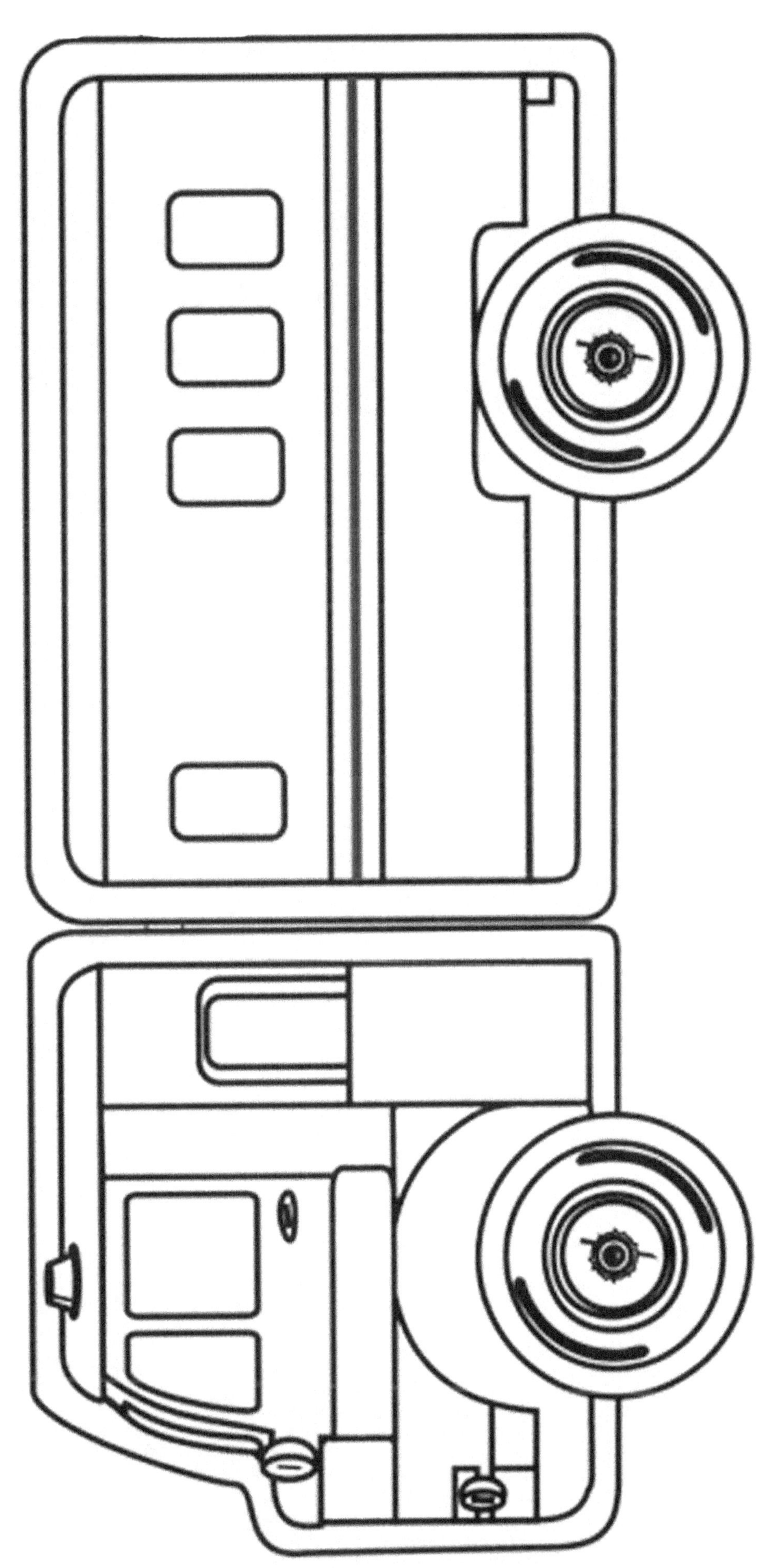

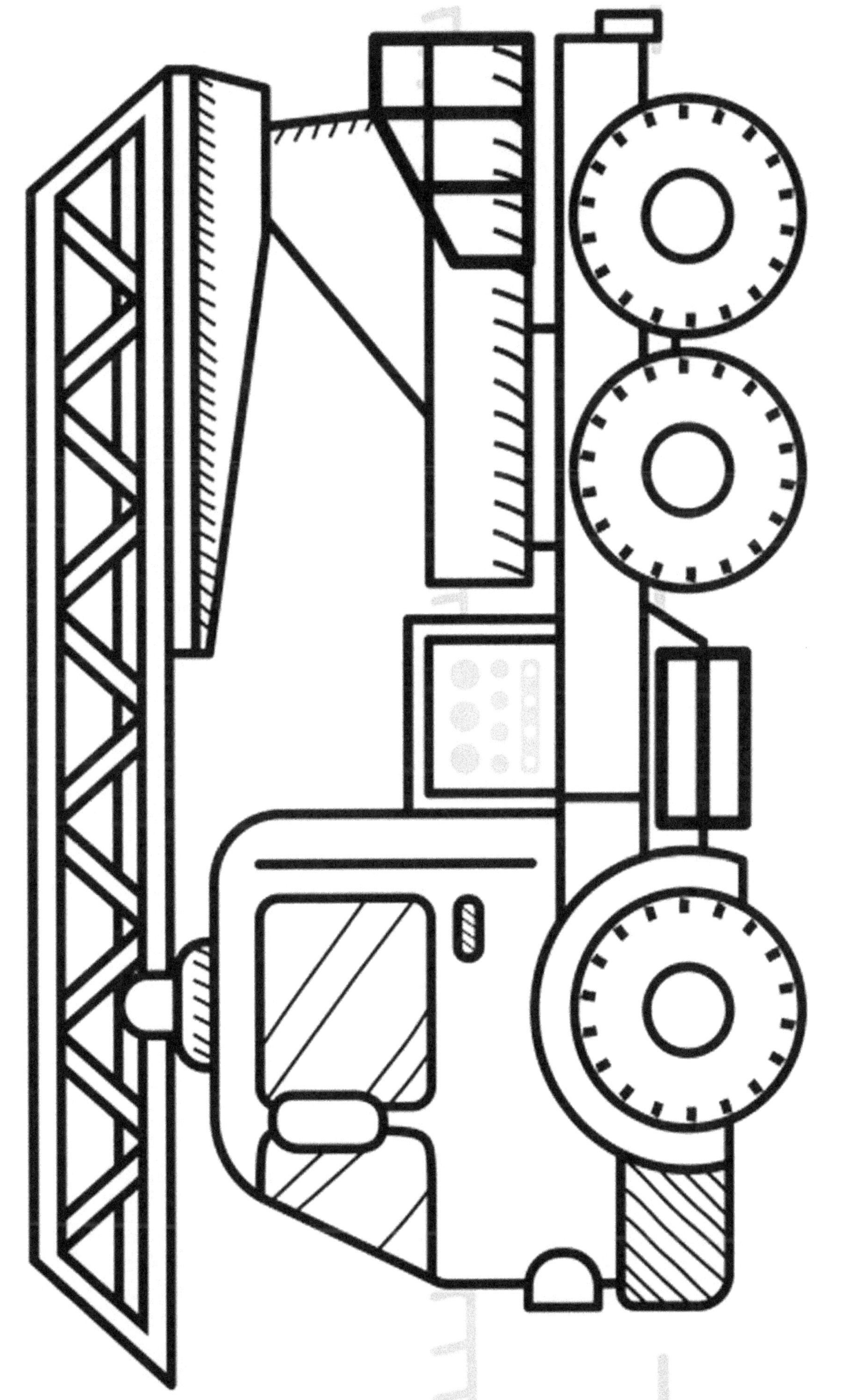

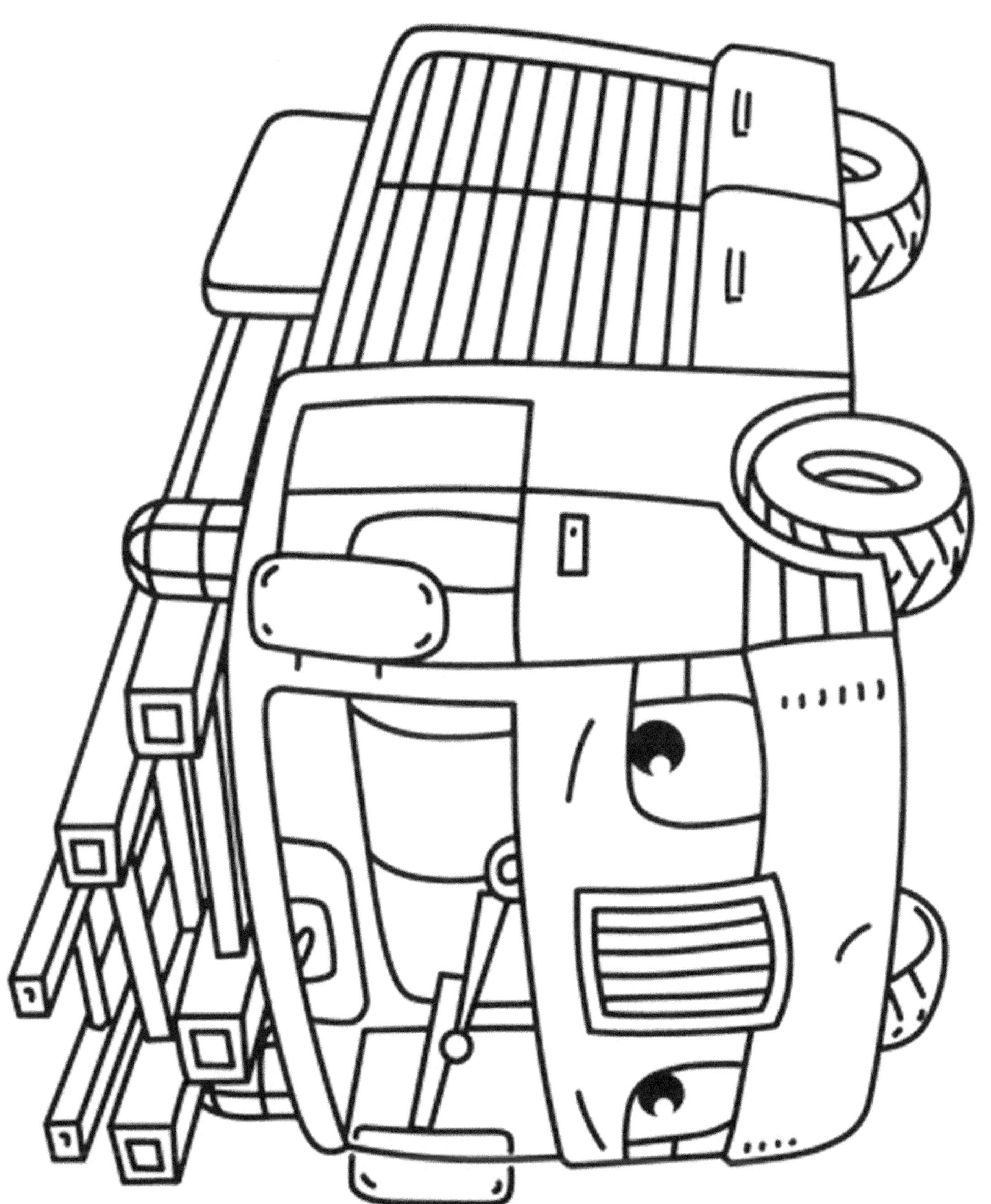

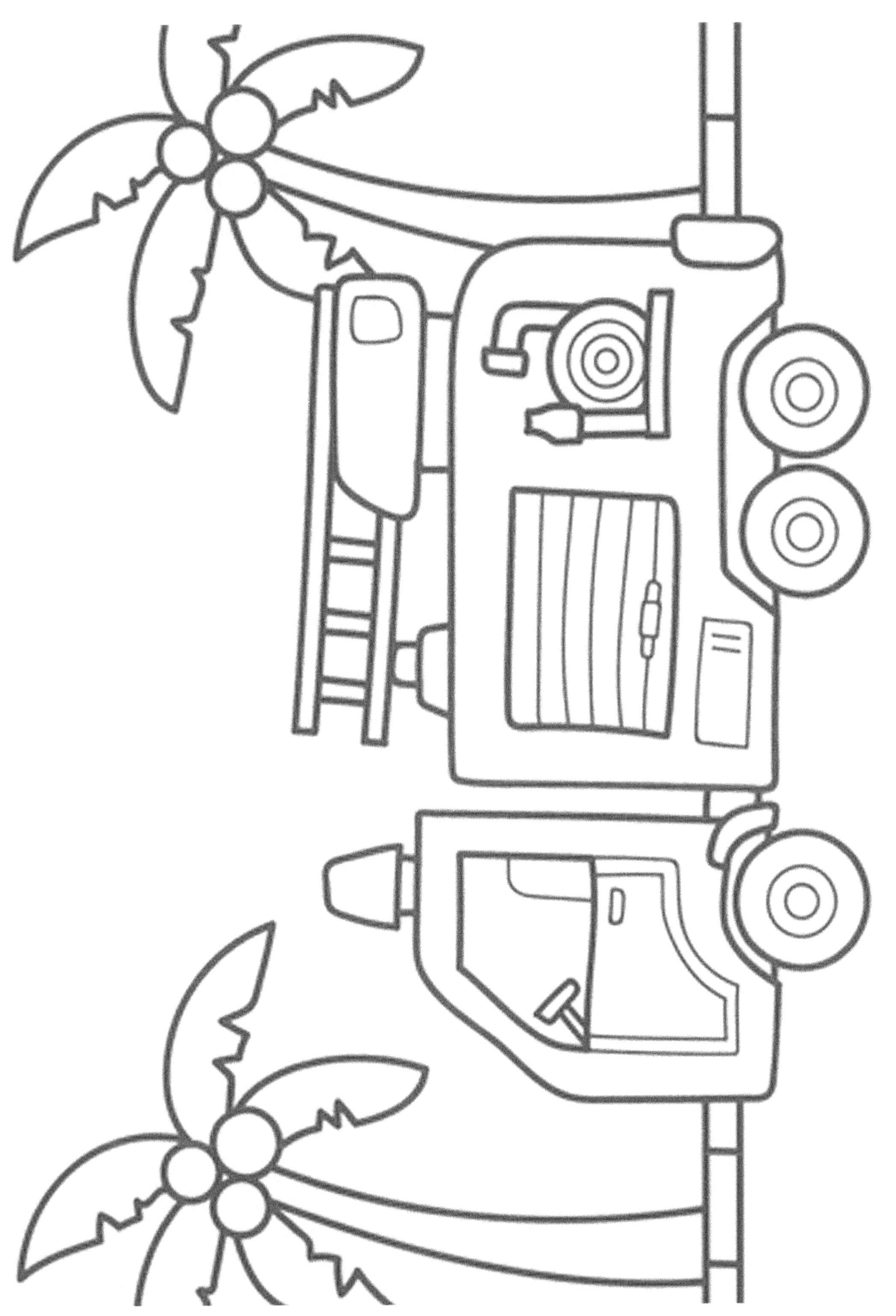

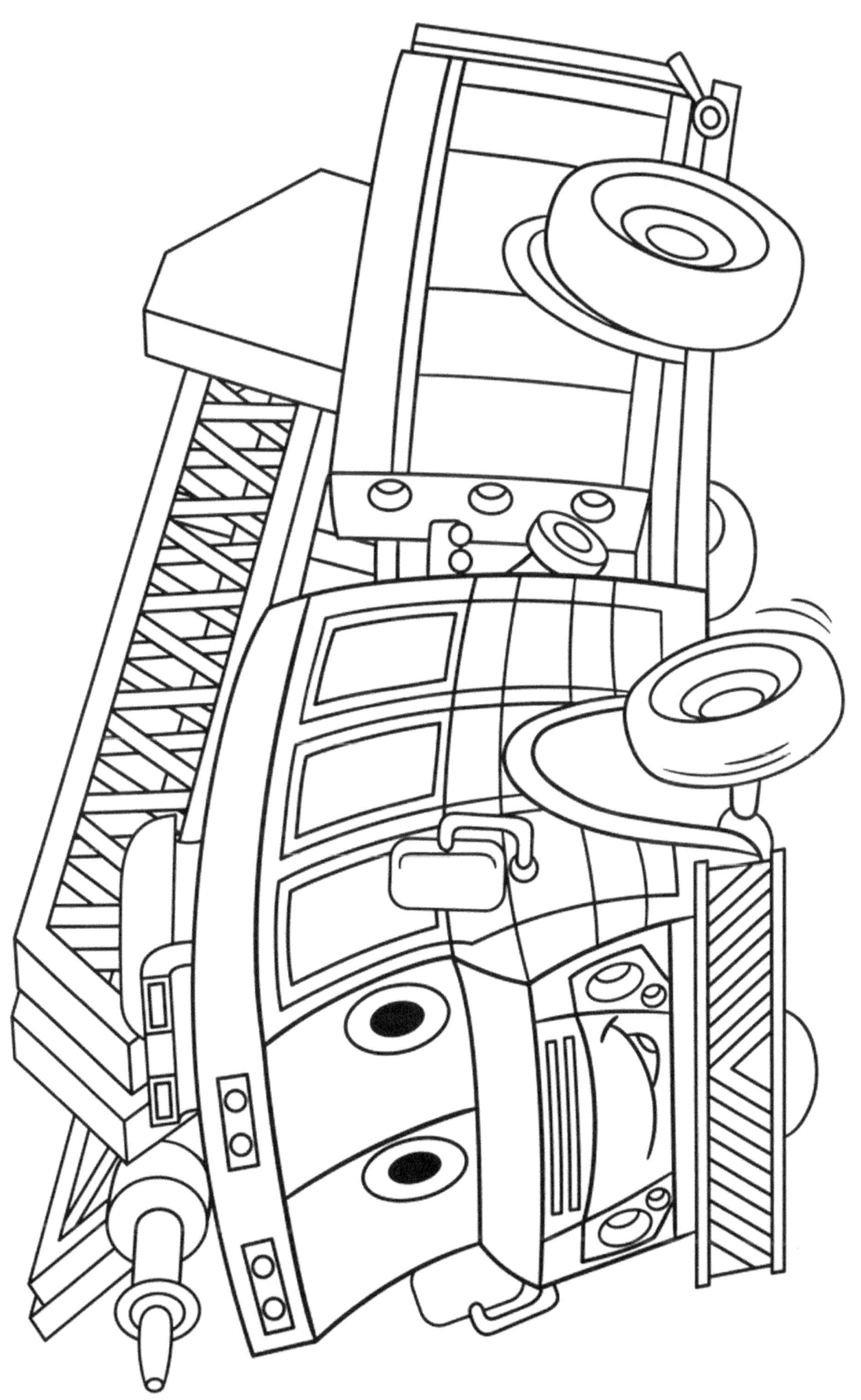

RESCUE

nee..
woah..
nee..
woah..

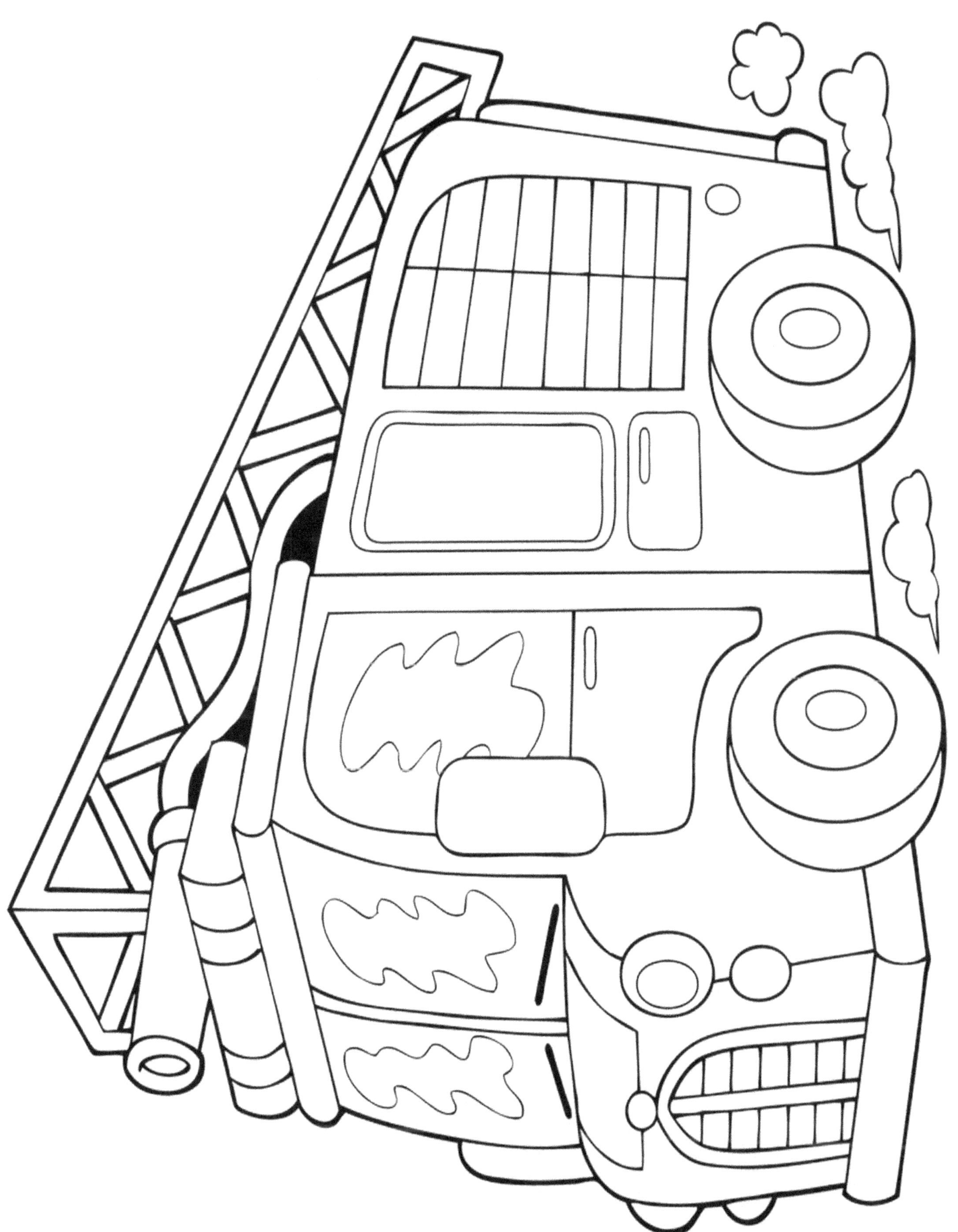

HEY!
WE WOULD LOVE
TO HEAR FROM YOU.

PLEASE LEAVE "**Pixelart Studio**" A REVIEW. YOUR FEEDBACKS AND OPINION CAN HELP US TO CREAT BETTER PRODUCTS FOR YOU.

COLORING BOOK..

Thank You!